Taking Care of Myself

Managing Friendships

By Meg Gaertner

level 2
little blue readers

www.littlebluehousebooks.com

Little Blue House is distributed by North Star Editions:
sales@northstareditions.com | 888-417-0195

Produced for Little Blue House by Red Line Editorial.

Photographs ©: Shutterstock Images, cover, 4, 6–7, 9, 14–15, 21 (top), 21 (bottom), 24 (top right), 24 (bottom left); iStockphoto, 10–11, 12, 17, 18, 22–23, 24 (top left), 24 (bottom right)

Library of Congress Control Number: 2021916813

ISBN
978-1-64619-494-0 (hardcover)
978-1-64619-521-3 (paperback)
978-1-64619-572-5 (ebook pdf)
978-1-64619-548-0 (hosted ebook)

Printed in the United States of America
Mankato, MN
012022

About the Author

Meg Gaertner enjoys reading, writing, dancing, and being outside. She lives in Minnesota.

Table of Contents

friends

Being a Good Friend

Friends have fun together.

They are kind and helpful to one another.

Certain skills help people make and keep friends.

Take turns while talking with your friends. Listen when they are talking. This shows you care about them.

Ask your friends questions.
This shows you are
interested in them.
You can ask about their
favorite games.
You can ask if they
have pets.

pet

Share toys with your friends at playtime. Take turns choosing the games. This way, everyone gets to have fun.

toys

yelling

Trouble

Sometimes friends do not agree.
You might get mad at your friends.
If so, do not hit them or yell.

Instead, walk away and take a break.
Breathe slowly and count to ten.
Wait until you feel peaceful again.

Then go back to
your friends.
Calmly tell them how
you feel.
You can fix the
problem together.
You can keep being
good friends.

Saying Sorry

Everyone makes mistakes sometimes. Maybe you have hurt a friend's feelings. If so, say you are sorry.

Saying sorry shows that you care.
It is also a promise.
You promise to try to be kinder next time.

Good friends listen and take turns. They share their feelings and say sorry. These skills take practice. But you can be a good friend.

Glossary

friends

toys

pet

yelling

Index